Series/Number 04-013

Recruitment and Incentive Patterns among Grassroots Republican Officials: Continuity and Change in Two States

THOMAS H. ROBACK
*Virginia Polytechnic Institute and
State University*

 SAGE PUBLICATIONS / Beverly Hills / London

For information address:

SAGE PUBLICATIONS, INC.
275 South Beverly Drive
Beverly Hills, California 90212

SAGE PUBLICATIONS LTD
St George's House / 44 Hatton Garden
London EC1N 8ER

International Standard Book Number **0-8039-0398-7**

Library of Congress Catalog Card No. **74-75547**

FIRST PRINTING

When citing a professional paper, please use the proper form. Remember to cite the
correct Sage Professional Paper series title and include the paper number. One of the
two following formats can be adapted (depending on the style manual used):

(1) NAGEL, S. S. (1973) "Comparing Elected and Appointed Judicial Systems."
Sage Professional Papers in American Politics, 1, 04-001. Beverly Hills, and London:
Sage Pubns.

OR

(2) Nagel, Stuart S. 1973. *Comparing Elected and Appointed Judicial Systems.* Sage
Professional Papers in American Politics, vol. 1, series no. 04-001. Beverly Hills and
London: Sage Publications.

CONTENTS

Recruitment and Incentive Patterns among Grassroots Republican Officials: Continuity and Change in Two States

THOMAS H. ROBACK
Virginia Polytechnic Institute and
  State University

Party leadership at the local level has undergone increasing analysis by investigators interested in understanding the nature of participation in political organizations. This growing body of literature generally has examined the relationships between the social characteristics, political activities and incentives for participation, organizational role definitions and recruitment patterns of grassroots activists at but single points in time. (See, for example, the following studies: Althoff and Patterson, 1966; Costantini and Craik, 1969; Crotty, 1967, 1968; Cutright and Rossi, 1958; Eldersveld, 1964; Flinn and Wirt, 1965; Hirschfield et al., 1962; Patterson, 1963; Pomper, 1965; and Rossi and Cutright, 1961.) The nature of development and change in the leadership cadre and organizational structure of local parties over time has not been examined systematically in either theoretical or empirical form. This tendency is not unique to the study of local parties and reflects the general direction of a good deal of social science research. However, this dearth of developmental research on grassroots parties can be viewed as especially important when viewed in light of the rap-

AUTHOR'S NOTE: *Some of the data in this manuscript originally appeared in a paper (with Philip L. Martin and Donald Lacy) presented at the 1971 Annual Meeting of the Southern Political Science Association, Gatlinburg, Tennessee, November 11-13. I wish to thank Philip L. Martin for permission to use the 1966 data. The Republican County Chairmen of Virginia and West Virginia likewise deserve thanks for their participation.*

id political and partisan change that has occurred in a number of Southern and Border states over the past decade. The development of persistent and successful Republican competition in these regions is no longer a cause for astonishment. (See, for example: Seagull, 1970; Grassmuck, 1964.) Consequently, an examination of the political and social sources of recruitment and activism of local party leaders provides a way to observe the nature of local Republican organizational development. It is this often unstable phenomenon of continuity and change in the patterns of recruitment and activism of grassroots Republican leaders in these locales that provides the major descriptive focus of this investigation.

THEORETICAL NOTIONS ABOUT RECRUITMENT AND INCENTIVES FOR ACTIVISM

The identification of who fills political roles and why certain people fill them at the expense of others is a central concern of party recruitment studies. This body of research has examined both the recruitment of party activists into leadership roles and the process of selection of candidates for public office (Barber, 1965; Bowman and Boynton, 1966a; Browning, 1968; Jacob, 1962; Kesselman, 1973; Patterson and Boynton, 1969; Seligman, 1961; Snowiss, 1966; Ziegler and Baer, 1968). A smaller body of research has investigated recruiters, recruitment groups, and the interaction between recruiters and candidates (Hunt and Pendley, 1972; Schwartz, 1969; Watts, 1968).

Another closely related series of investigations examines the incentives and motivations for becoming active in party work and leadership. Clark and Wilson (1961) maintain that individual susceptibility to organizational incentives are major reasons for initial sustained activity in political and other types of organizations (see also: Althoff and Brady, 1972; Althoff and Patterson, 1966; Conway and Feigart, 1968; Eldersveld, 1964; Gluck, 1972; Ippolito, 1969a; Marvick and Nixon, 1961; Sorauf, 1968; Wilson, 1962). Their widely known system of incentives falls in three categories: material or tangible incentives; purposive incentives which derive from the stated ends and suprapersonal goals of the organization, e.g., the ideological and public policy program of a political party; and solidary incentives which result from association with others and "include such rewards as socializing, congenialty, and sense of group membership and identification, the status resulting from membership, fun and conviviality, and the maintenance of social distinctions and so on" (Clark and

Wilson, 1961: 134-35).

In this investigation, the availability for recruitment into a party leadership role is conceptualized as partially being a function of social characteristics and organizational incentives. Party activists with particular social backgrounds that are considered desirable according to some normative group consensus can be recruited directly into a leadership position (see Alford and Scoble, 1968; Bowman and Boynton, 1966a; Prewitt, 1970). Some of the research on primary groups point out that social attributes have indirect effects on the degree of organizational activism because social background influences the socialization of ideological content and intensity, differential sensitivity to organizational incentives and organizational role perceptions (see Hofstetter, 1972; McCloskey and Dahlgren, 1959; Salisbury, 1965-66; Sears, 1969). Social and political background form the initial series of agents that affect the probabilities associated with activism. The later and more immediate factors for involvment consist of either: self-generated stimuli which usually result from the matching of party incentive systems and personal goals and motives; or external factors like the persuasion of party activists or friends and the openness of the party organization. The theoretical emphasis in this investigation essentially is in agreement with Sorauf's (1968: 91) conclusion that "recruitment, in whatever form, is a matching of the motives and goals of the individual with the incentives and expectations of the party organization. The immediate act of recruitment is either the catalyst or the occasion for the matching."[1] The nature and interaction of these factors (including political ambition as a source of motivation) comprise the primary conceptual focus of this study.

All of these factors operate within or between two basic levels of analysis. At the micro level, the attributes and backgrounds that are related to "general" political participation among individuals and groups are considered most crucial in explaining which kinds of people become party activists and leaders. The second level views party recruitment and activism from a systemic, i.e., macro, perspective and considers it part of a community and organizational process in which the party structure interacts with the political and social environment.[2] A complete treatment of party recruitment and activism obviously should examine concepts at both of these levels of analysis. While not attempting to construct or test a complete theoretical model of recruitment, attention to the rationale behind the conceptual and empirical linkage of individual political and social variables and organizational-contextual factors provides the backdrop for this study.

Consequently, measures of the following participatory and community level factors are used to examine aggregate patterns of activism and recruitment:

(1) social attributes and background;

(2) reasons for initial political involvement and incentives for entry into the party organization (including incentives used to attract and recruit candidates for office);

(3) political ambition and career aspirations; and

(4) self-definitions of the county chairman role.

When appropriate, these factors are examined under conditions related to degree of urbanization and inter-party competition present in the political environment.[3]

THE STUDY DESIGN AND SETTINGS

This study compares the similarities and differences between two sets of Republican county chairmen who served in 1966 and 1970 in Virginia and West Virginia. The names of the chairmen were taken from lists provided by Republican state officials and data were gathered by means of a mail questionnaire. The return rate for Virginia was 104 responses from 109 units in 1966 (94%) and 104 responses from 116 units in 1970 (90%). For West Virginia there were 40 returns from 55 units in 1966 (73%) and 36 completions from 55 units in 1970 (65%). It should be noted that the data reflect Virginia's unique distinction between its 95 counties and 38 independent cities, some of which have independent party organizations. The number of these cities adopting independent status (in mostly urban areas) is subject to change from year to year and their boundaries also fluctuate over time as a result of consolidation and annexation. The initial mailings in both time periods were followed by postcard reminders and a second wave of questionnaires.[4]

In order to control unwanted, additive effects, incumbent chairmen from 1970 (except where noted) have not been included in most portions of the analysis. An examination of initial recruitment and incentive patterns makes it important to point out how the new chairmen in 1970 compare to the chairmen from 1966. The importance of measuring similarities or differences between the organizational cadres by means of creating mutually exclusive categories is especially appropriate when particular social characteristics (like age and length of residence) are involved. Because the differences in the social characteristics and incentive patterns of both the incumbent and new chairmen from 1966 were minimal, separate analysis of these groups will not be undertaken. Also, the matter of the retention or deletion of certain types of chairmen during the time period will be explored as a datum that may reflect another dimension of change. However, it should be noted that the unit of analysis in this study is the characteristics of individual party leaders as aggregated by time and state and the intent here is not the measurement of change per se in the activity or structure of the local organizations themselves.

Although the comparative study of state and regional variations in political style and culture has not been conclusive, it would appear worthwhile to examine party organizational recruitment and motivation with this geographical and cultural diversity in mind (see Patterson, 1968; and Elazar, 1966). Patterson points out that:

> The states are political sub-systems which . . . crucially affect the persistence of the national political system . . . yet the states can be treated for analytical purposes as relatively independent political systems with political cultures at least somewhat distinctive to themselves . . . The generality of these kinds of differences are unknown (but) no one would expect the American political culture to be uniformly distributed spatially; our evidence is adequate enough to show that the political culture of Mississippi is not the same as that of Iowa [Patterson, 1968: 195].

If there are interstate variations in political orientations, it would be expected that party organizational styles also might vary and this notion provides a guide for this investigation into Republican party activism in Virginia and West Virginia.

In the recent past, the measurement of the degree of competition in the party systems of Virginia and West Virginia generally has resulted in their being categorized as "modified one-party Democratic." (For a discussion of classification criteria see: Ranney, 1965; Schlesinger, 1955; Wright, 1971.) Recently, however, the Republican parties in each state have shown increasing degrees of electoral success to the extent that a more appropriate classification (in varying degrees in each state) would be that of "transitional party system." A definition of this type of party system holds that:

> By a transitional political party within the American context, it is meant a party that is increasing its share of the popular vote and its probabilities of winning elective offices. These factors are related to, and reflected in a party that actively organizes and competes with the majority party on a more inclusive basis, is

represented by a systematic geographical expansion of its activities, and on a more intensive basis, is competitive at a series of
levels within a given locality [Crotty, 1967: 681, note 25].

An understanding of the evolution of the GOP in these two contigu-
ous political systems requires recognition of the fact that West Virginia was the Unionist rump of Virginia and the indirect creation of the
Civil War while Confederate Virginia until recently has remained in
the control of post-Reconstruction one-party Democratic dominance.
Thus, the much earlier Republican development and success in West
Virginia was a corollary of historical circumstance while Virginia's recent Republican success has been more gradual and orderly. Viable
Republican competition in West Virginia began in a strong position
but has undergone long-term cyclical periods of retreat and advance
that leave it approximately abreast of a surging GOP in Virginia.[5]
Because of these factors, both transitional party systems provide a
unique background within which to examine party organizational
leadership. The primary emphasis on analysis of the data will be on
intrastate variation between the county chairmen of 1966 and 1970 in
each state. The comparison of interstate similarities and differences
for the same time period will comprise the other analytic focus.

PATTERNS OF GRASSROOTS RECRUITMENT AND ACTIVISM: ANALYSIS OF THE DATA

Social Backgrounds of Grassroots Leaders

The major assumption in this section is that an analysis of basic
social variables is important to the formation of a complete description of the type of individuals and the reasons why individuals become
active in local party organizations. Education, age, length of residence, and occupation are to be examined but the sharing of several
other attributes is worthy of mention. All the chairmen in both states
are white and they are predominantly male (with two chairwomen
found in Virginia in 1970). They tend to be products of small-town
environments with the mean falling in places where the population is
7,500 or less.

It has been pointed out that because of its weakness in predominantly Democratic states (especially in the South), the Republican Party until recently has been a relatively "open" organization. As
a result, the officials of local and state party bureaucracies have

tended to attract and recruit individuals who are unwilling to put in much apprenticeship (Crotty, 1967: 672-673). Moreover, from studies made of party chairmen in Oklahoma, North Carolina, New Jersey, as well as Kansas and Wisconsin (Patterson, 1963; Crotty, 1967; Pomper, 1965), the majority party has been found to attract the so-called "better people" of higher social status while the minority party attracts more "marginal" social types.[6] Thus, it can be hypothesized that the nature of recruitment into party roles depends in part on mutual attraction between the strength of the party (majority versus minority) and the social, demographic, cultural and residential longevity and visibility of prospective recruits. In line with the notion of transition developed earlier, as the minority party becomes more competitive, it should be better able to recruit individuals into the party organization who are more integrated into and reflective of the local political and social context. As a minority party's fortunes rise, the social characteristics of its local officials should begin to approximate those of local leaders found in many competitive or majority party settings. The evidence in Virginia and West Virginia is mixed (to be expected for only a four and one-half year interval) and leads to the acceptability of the hypothesis only with qualifications and often idiosyncratic explanations for the patterns of social attributes in each state. Before examining each social variable, a brief a priori overview of the findings may be instructive. The data (especially in Virginia) produce some evidence that shows that on the whole the Republican leaders in these transitional party systems often do not conform to those characteristics that have been attributed to minority chairmen in other states. That is, in many instances, these minority Republican leaders resemble the majority party activists found in studies of the other states mentioned above. Moreover, the earlier group of chairmen from 1965-66 also conform to this "majority" pattern especially where education and occupation are concerned.[7] Thus, the amount of change in the social backgrounds of the chairmen recruited in both states from 1966 to 1970 is not very dramatic. The question of whether earlier groups of pre-1966 Republican chairmen more accurately fit the mold of minority party activists is likely but empirically untestable in this study. It is clear that by 1966 involvement in the minority party in both states was more attractive to higher status people than one might have expected.

The notion of "transitional lag" can be offered as a tentative and partial explanation of this phenomenon. It may be that qualitative shifts in general party cadre recruitment (as also influenced by the increasing share of the vote that the minority party mobilizes as it moves to transitional status) were pre-dated by the recruitment and subsequent activity of a variant of what Marvick (1968) has called "core cadre."[8] In Virginia and West Virginia, some of these more highly motivated leaders with high social status may have been attracted to the Republican party at an earlier stage for diverse reasons of their own which also could have included their perception of its probable emergence as a competitive local or state alternative. After all, the historical foundation and viability of the GOP in West Virginia should have been no stranger to potential political activists. Also, in the peripheral Southern state of Virginia, presidential successes from 1952 to 1960 and the retention of several "safe" Republican Congressional seats during the late 1950's and early 1960's gave the Republican party a good deal of visibility and respectability. Consequently, it is possible that the achievement of "transitional" party system status in the electoral sense with its bonus of attracting grassroots supporters, lagged behind the earlier recruitment of individuals who saw the possibility of the transition before it occurred and felt no social constraints about identifying with the "minority" party. However, there are some modest increases in recruiting chairmen of higher social status during the time interval and these will be noted in the following analysis.[9] Although almost none of the within-state percentage differences are statistically significant, the direction and modest changes are considered at least consistent with the previous theoretical discussion and notable in light of the length of the time interval.

As expected, the county chairmen as a group are better educated and hold higher status occupations than the general population.[10] Table 1 examines the social attributes of both sets of chairmen in both time periods. Virginia is represented by a relatively stable pattern from 1966 to 1970 with a slight decline in the lower (high school or less) educated category and a slight increase in graduate degrees. In West Virginia, there are comparable increases among the more highly educated but no large change in the unusually high representation in the high school or less category.[11] In summary, the major interstate educational differences between the chairmen are found in the higher number of lower educated chairmen in West Virginia and, conversely, in the greater number of chairmen with professional or graduate degrees in Virginia. However, the most general finding is that the chairmen from both states are slightly better educated than their counterparts of 1966. Given the unusual number of highly educated officials in the minority party cadre from 1966, this only gradual increase is to be expected.

The examination of the differences in the age distributions of the county chairmen is another way to describe grassroots party recruitment in these two states.[12] Although the pattern is more pronounced in Virginia, a modest shift can be discerned in both states from recruiting the relatively young or old to those in the middle years from 35 to 54 (see Table 1). Crotty (1967: 671-673) has pointed out that before the period of Republican development in many parts of the South, the attraction of "instant clout" often resulted in socially marginal party officials who were either quite young or quite old. Although the ages of the 1966 chairmen in Virginia tend to be clustered around the middle-age categories, the increase in the 35 to 54 category by 1970 is still significant. There are gradual declines both

TABLE 1
SOCIAL CHARACTERISTICS OF REPUBLICAN COUNTY
CHAIRMEN BY STATE AND YEAR
(in percentages)

Characteristic	Virginia 1966 (N=101)	Virginia 1970 (N=86)[a]	West Virginia 1966 (N=40)	West Virginia 1970 (N=30)[a]
Education				
High school or less	17%	12%	30%	25%
Some college	27	23	30	25
College degree	28	32	33	38
Professional - graduate degrees	28	33	7	12
Total	100%	100%	100%	100%
Age				
25-34[b]	28%	17%	13%	6%
35-44	37	40	22	34
45-54	18*	32	32	30
55-64	8	8	18	18
65 or over	9	3	15	12
Total	100%	100%	100%	100%
Years of Residence				
1-5	16%	7%	5%	-%
6-10	18	8	8	6
11-20	19	23	10	8
over 20 but not all of life	17	24	27	25
all of life	30	38	50	61
Total	100%	100%	100%	100%
Occupation				
Professional	39%	45%	37%	37%
Farm owner-operator	15	8	8	6
Manager-business-sales official	24	29	30	41
Craftsmen, foremen, operatives	10	8	17	11
Other (clerical, clerk, retired, government)	12	10	8	5
Total	100%	100%	100%	100%

[a]Incumbents not included.
[b]Includes one 1966 Virginia chairman who was under 25.

*Denotes statistical significance at .05 for within-state percentage differences between years based on the chi-square distribution and the population N's for each time period. The table of significant percentage differences used to evaluate the data in this table can be found in Buchanan (1970: 87). Use of the .10 level would have resulted several other significant percentage differences.

among the very young and very old categories which probably indicates some new recruitment patterns in some locales where Republican strength is increasing. In West Virginia, the shifts in the age distribution reflect a slight tendency away from chairmen under thirty-four, an increase in the 34 to 44 lower middle-age group and stability in the 45- to 65-over categories. The greater longevity of viable local Republican organizations in West Virginia has already been mentioned and may be a partial indicator of why there has not been a greater injection of new, more "middle-aged" blood into the chairmenship posts between 1966 and 1970. Since West Virginia has been very much a minority party since 1932, there may be no takers willing to oust longstanding "patronage Republican" organizations (particularly in Democratic county strongholds) that are often controlled by an older set of cadre (Fenton, 1957). Indeed, the most striking interstate age difference between the chairmen lies in this preponderance of older chairmen in the West Virginia party.

Along with the fact that more better educated and middle-aged party cadre should appear as a transitional party system emerges, there also should be a commensurate increase in those who have more established residential roots in their communities. Newly recruited officials in this context often will share all three of these characteristics but residential longevity is important and deserves separate mention.

Knowledge about an individual's length of residence in a particular area can reflect the degree of his social integration in that area and be helpful in explaining the direction of his political activism. In the case of this variable, the relationship between transitional Republican development and recruitment pattern may be "causally" reversible. It might be the case that a party becomes competitive by initially recruiting enough "solid citizens" until a "threshold" is passed resulting in a politically effective and socially acceptable local party organization.

Table 1 shows that the percentage of chairmen living in their counties 20 years or more goes from 47 to 62% in Virginia and from 77 to 86% in West Virginia over the four year period. Once again, there were a considerable number of chairmen from 1966 in both states who had established residential longevity but the increases over time are not insubstantial. The general picture reflects a tendency toward increased recruitment of officials who are more deeply rooted in their communities.[13] The major interstate finding is that the longer-established party organizations in West Virginia appear to have had earlier and more pronounced success in recruiting native sons willing to stake their social and political futures with the Republican Party.

Occupation is the final measure of social status to be examined and further illustrates the relatively high social status of the local party officials. As compared to the general population, a pronounced degree of upper status occupations are found among the chairmen in both states.[14] Crotty (1967: 676) describes a well-known explanation of why particular occupations contribute such a disproportionate share of political activists:

> . . . it is argued that high socio-economic status reflected in high status occupations connotes the achievement and success, a bargainable commodity in seeking political support, insures the possession of the fundamental personal and verbal skills, correlates with a high degree of political interest and realism, and offers the opportunity to associate with people who can expedite the mechanics of political entry and who have access to the necessary financial resources.[15]

In Virginia, the within-state differences over the time period show steady increases in the direction of recruiting higher-status chairmen but again are not substantial due to the already large group of businessmen and professionals already in office in 1966. However, there is a noticeable decline among farm owners and operators during this period. This decline may partially be due to the perceptions by Republican leaders of the increasing urbanization of the state.[16] In West Virginia, several changes take place between 1966 and 1970. There is an increase of chairmen in the manager-sales category (from 30% to 41%) and the relatively high but expected blue-collar representation in 1966 dips slightly from 17% to 11%. In both states, the number of chairmen in low status, "fringe" occupations shows a slight decline. In Virginia, within the upper status occupations, more professionals were recruited over the time span while in West Virginia the greatest white-collar increase occurred among businessmen.

Table 2 portrays some generational differences between the occupations of the county chairmen and their fathers. This table can also be interpreted as an indirect indicator of upward occupational, i.e., social, mobility. The overriding message in this table is that as far as social status is concerned, the Republican Party in West Virginia has been a more wide open affair than in Virginia during periods of organizational recruitment. It is likely that the acceptance of mining and union organizational affiliation as a suitable social prerequisite for party activism may account for a portion of this large generational status gap between the occupations of the chairmen and their fathers.

It is clear that the social status of the county chairmen is much higher than the level of their fathers. The fathers holding white-collar jobs in Virginia are decidedly more numerous than their West Virginia counterparts for both years. Consequently, there has been a much greater tendency for the chairmen in West Virginia to be more upwardly mobile (and in the process, begin to change the demographic character of the party cadre).

The relationships between, on the one hand, size of community and party dominance (as environmental characteristics of the counties) and, on the other, occupation, generally uphold the direction of the original occupation distribution. Although the data are not shown, from 1966 to 1970, both states either increased or maintained the levels of recruitment of chairmen from the professional, managerial and sales categories in rural, lesser urban and urban counties.[17] Both states show steady increases in the lesser urban, i.e., suburban, areas, which indicates the increasing legitimacy of the Republican Party in these locales. Also, an effort appears to have been made to increase the number of higher status chairmen in the traditionally

TABLE 2

OCCUPATIONAL STATUS OF REPUBLICAN
COUNTY CHAIRMEN AND THEIR FATHERS
(in percentages)

	Percent Holding White Collar Occupations[a]			
	Virginia 1966	Virginia 1970	West Virginia 1966	West Virginia 1970
County Chairmen	67%	75%	69%	74%
Fathers of Chairmen	49	50	27	35
Percentage point difference	18*	25*	42*	39*
N =	(70)	(72)	(28)	(25)

[a]Includes the following: professionals, managers, business proprietors, sales and government service.

*Percentage difference significant at the .05 level using the chi-square distribution and the population N's for each time period.

Democratic urban areas of West Virginia. These shifts indicate that the Republican local organizations are recruiting more of these people as chairmen throughout both states but especially in the centers of increasing population.

The relationship over time between differential party dominance[18] in the counties and this same "white collar" occupational category is shown in Table 3. Republican county chairmen of high occupational status are increasing in both states. This finding is expected in the Republican-dominant and competitive counties as a function of the increasing acceptance of the GOP as a solid partisan organization that can win elections. In Democratic-dominant counties, the Republican county organizations (depending on their "openness"), may provide bright, upwardly mobile "young men on the make" with opportunities to be recruited rather quickly into responsible local party positions. The lure of rapid advancement in an underdog but perhaps promising political milieu could be a real factor pushing these professional and business types over the "threshold" into party activism.[19] Although, there are no real differences between the chairmen in terms of the relationship between party dominance and occupation, the uniformity of the increase of upper-status chairmen may reflect the transition of the Republican Party in many locales from a deviant to a more legitimate organ of partisan identification and activism.

In summation, the county chairmen of Virginia and West Virginia were unique in that in both 1966 and 1970, they were recruited from

TABLE 3

OCCUPATIONAL STATUS OF CHAIRMEN
AND DEGREE OF COUNTY PARTY DOMINANCE
BY STATE AND YEAR
(in percentages)

County Dominance Pattern	Percent Holding White Collar Occupations					
	Virginia 1966	Virginia 1970	D*	West Virginia 1966	West Virginia 1970	D*
Republican-Dominant	(22) 61%	(26) 75%	14%	(12) 60%	(11) 70%	10%
Competitive	(17) 66	(30) 74	8	(15) 75	(15) 83	8
Democratic-Dominant	(61) 65	(34) 77	12	(10) 67	(6) 77	10

*Percentage point difference across rows.

more upper status and more socially "legitimate" community strata than were other minority party chairmen in other states in other periods. However, there were modest increases in upper status social attributes as the Republican Party in both states became more competitive. The two political systems often translated this general development in idiosyncratic terms, but the tenor of it appears logical and consistent in terms of the discussion of the changes in social attributes of local party officials expected in transitional party systems.

Political Backgrounds

The political backgrounds of party chairmen concerning the familial roots of their political and partisan involvement provide additional factors that are useful in understanding grassroots recruitment. A good portion of the literature in political participation and socialization emphasizes the general importance of the level of parental political activity as an indicator of the subsequent activity of offspring. The political activity of the chairmen's parents has remained relatively stable over the time period (see Table 4). In Virginia, less than half of the chairmen could have acquired their interest in politics and party activities from their parents. The parents who have previous political

TABLE 4

POLITICAL ACTIVITY OF PARENTS
OF COUNTY CHAIRMEN BY STATE AND YEAR
(in percentages)

	Virginia 1966	Virginia 1970	West Virginia 1966	West Virginia 1970
One or more family members politically active N =	42% (101)	47% (86)	63% (40)	61% (30)
Party Identification of Active Parents				
One Republican	36%	28%	31%	46%
Both Republican	40	34	55	43
One Democrat	17	30	5	6
Both Democrat	7	8	9	5
Total	100%	100%	100%	100%
N =	(50)	(45)	(29)	(25)

background are more numerous in West Virginia than in Virginia.

The party identification of the chairmen's parents who were politically active is predominantly Republican. In Virginia, there has been one significant change during the five year period. In 1970, 62% of the chairmen had one or both active parents affiliated with the Republican Party, whereas 76% of these politically involved parents in 1966 had been or were active in the GOP. The decrease in the proportion of chairmen coming from Republican family backgrounds and the increase of chairmen whose parents were active Democrats also is interesting in light of recent findings on mass voting patterns in the South.[20] In West Virginia, the party affiliation of the active parents tends to be more heavily Republican but there is no comparable increase of Democratic parents over the time span. Although this study has no data on the fathers of non-politicians, these findings indicate support of the common notion that parental political activity develops positive *expectations* about the likelihood of political achievement and affiliation within the male child. This logic holds that increased visibility and opportunity should lead to a greater probability of eventual recruitment and entrance into the party (see also: Prewitt, 1965; Milbrath, 1965).

Incentives for Activism

Individual motives[21] for participation in a political organization are closely tied to the incentives that the organization is able to offer. In most of its forms, recruitment is the matching of the motives and goals of the individual with the incentives and expectations of the party organization (see Sorauf, 1968: 92). The county chairmen were asked to respond to a list of incentives for initial activism in terms of their importance. The distribution for each incentive offered by the party organization is outlined in Table 5 while a more parsimonious index of the relative importance of each incentive category for the chairmen is presented in Table 6.

The *purposive* incentives rest at the top of the hierarchy of motivations for activism. Ideology and general civic duty as sources of motivations to affect government comprise an extremely high and durable indication of initial entry into Republican organizations in both states.[22] Of course, civic obligation is a socially acceptable motive and can mask other less acceptable motives. However, as Sorauf (1968: 89) points out, "often . . . it is an honest testament to the power of deeply-ingrained civic values. Those values rarely operate alone, but they do reinforce and provide important rationalization for other goals and motives."

Solidary incentives for party activism occupy the middle portion of this hierarchical comparison of motivations. These social rewards of politics are measured in a general way by the importance of party

TABLE 5

IMPORTANCE OF INCENTIVES FOR INITIAL
PARTY ACTIVISM BY STATE AND YEAR*
(in percentages)

Incentives	Virginia		West Virginia	
	1966	1970	1966	1970
Purposive:				
Concern with issues	98%	97%	100%	94%
Community obligation	94	96	97	86
Solidary:				
Strong party loyalty	84	73	92	91
Politics as way of life	60	65	64	66
Campaign action	46	53	33	68
Personal friend of candidate	30	36	47	50
Social contacts	17	23	15	26
Material:				
Furthering political ambitions	26	31	20	24
Involvement with influential				
people	15	20	15	27
Business reasons	8	14	13	25
N =	(102)	(86)	(40)	(30)

*In percentages of those to whom the incentive was "important" or "very important."

TABLE 6

THE IMPORTANCE OF PURPOSIVE, SOLIDARY
AND MATERIAL INCENTIVES BY STATE AND YEAR

Categories of Incentives	Virginia		West Virginia	
(Grand Mean Score)*	1966	1970	1966	1970
Purposive	1.62	1.21	1.24	1.46
Solidary	2.40	2.39	2.25	2.05
Material	2.87	2.60	2.83	2.57
N =	(102)	(86)	(40)	(30)

*The possible ratings are: (1) "very important"; (2) "somewhat important"; (3) "not too important"; and (4) "not important at all". By averaging the ratings across each incentive, the index scores were computed. Consequently, the higher the grand mean, the lower the incentive category in importance.

loyalty and the image of the party as a "way of life." These incentives receive considerable support in both states over the time period. Sorauf (1968: 89) points out the importance of the party per se as a type of personalized secondary group when he discusses loyalty as an incentive for activism:

> . . . the party becomes an end in itself. It retains the capacity for achieving the goals and rewards of politics, but at the same time its workers attach many of their loyalties and aspirations to it. The party's wins and losses become issues in and of themselves, and attacks on it are far more than attacks on its policies and activities.[23]

The rankings of more specific instances of solidary incentives show that campaign "fun and excitement" are cited next, followed by candidate friendship, and social contacts. About half of the Virginia chairmen in both years felt that the factor of being part of a campaign effort provided some motivation to enter the party organization. In West Virginia, the percentages go in opposite directions in both years. While only 33% perceived campaigning as an important factor in 1966, 68% saw it as a source of motivation in 1970.[24] Little difference over time was found in responses to personal contact and friendship with a candidate as motives for entrance into party activism. Social satisfactions appear to have secondary importance in the minds of the chairmen. The work and potential frustration attached to a grassroots leadership position may "weed out" low-activity partisans who initially were seeking some form of convivial camaraderie.

Material incentives form the least important category of activators for party involvement. The rewards associated with making "business contacts" or interacting with "influential people" are viewed as minor. The general notion of future political ambition is considered to be more important by the Virginia leaders but no substantial changes occur over time. The question of whether the decision to serve as county chairman might be based on the perception of the office as an interim position leading to better political opportunities will be examined later in more depth.[25]

As the summary scores in Table 6 indicate, the differences between the importance of incentive categories by state and year are relatively minor. For each state the ranking of the incentive categories was the same. The small variations in the importance attributed to each category of incentives that do appear are idiosyncratic and reveal the maintenance of continuity over the time interval. Once more, the 1966 and 1970 chairmen in both states tended to value and rank the incentives in the same order and with approximately the same degree of importance. The index scores reinforce the findings in Table 5 and show concisely that all four groups of chairmen ranked the incentive categories in the same declining order of importance—from purposive to solidary, on down to material. The grassroots officials from both states appear to be more highly motivated by civic obligation, public issues and party loyalty than by the lure of material gain or simple social contacts.[26] The differences both within and between the states, then, were slight and indicate a measure of commonality that expresses a rather strong and consistent ordering of the incentives among the Republican officials.

Incentives for Candidate Recruitment

A major way that grassroots leaders can affect the nature of the party organization is through involvement in both rank-and-file and candidate recruitment. The role of the county chairman as "recruiter" can be assessed partially by examining the incentives offered to prospective candidates to run for public office. By stressing impersonal, i.e., purposive, reasons and benefits in explaining to a candidate why he should enter a contest, the grassroots leader may selectively recruit candidates whose motivations and expectations are similar to his own. About one-half of the Virginia leaders and about three-fourths of the West Virginia leaders for both years had ever had to persuade, i.e., "draft," a candidate.[27]

Table 7 indicates that two of the impersonal reasons (build two-party system and citizen duty) are used to a high degree by the county chairmen. As the Republican Party has developed greater electoral strength from 1966 to 1970, the appeal of a viable two-party system in these locales appears to have attained more credibility as a realistic incentive for candidate recruitment. This emphasis upon these impersonal incentives parallels the tendency among the chairmen to cite purposive incentives as important goals for their own initial party activism. The personal inducement related to probable victory is also used widely to draft candidates. Party obligation (as a "turn one must take") and patronage benefits are not utilized widely in this "recruiter" role of the county chairmen. Other investigators have found that the general nature of incentives used to recruit candidates may reflect the motivational orientation of the recruiters as they attempt to keep their local orgaizations well represented in electoral contests.[28] However, no evidence of such a direct relationship was found in this study.

Political Career Ambitions

An examination of the county chairmanship in the political opportunity structure and the nature of specific ambitions toward a political career provides other ways to describe recruitment and incentive systems.[29] The extent to which the county chairmanship office represents an attractive opportunity or a terminal headache for its occupants should help us understand the types of people who lead the local parties. One indicator of the career patterns of the officials is tenure in office. It already has been mentioned that there was substantial turnover between 1966 and 1970 in both states. In 1970, 14% of the Virginia officials and 19% of the West Virginia officials had served in 1966. This high turnover rate indicates that the county chairmanship position is not a culminating one. Given the probability that many of the chairmen received the initial encouragement to serve

TABLE 7

INCENTIVES STRESSED IN RECRUITING CANDIDATES FOR PUBLIC OFFICE[a]
(in percentages)

Incentives[b]	Virginia 1966	Virginia 1970	West Virginia 1966	West Virginia 1970
Impersonal:				
Build two-party system	88%	98%	87%	97%
Sense of citizen duty	70	77	55	58
Party obligation and duty	22	11	19	19
Personal:				
High probability of winning	75	74	48	88
Patronage appeal (win or lose)	4	6	3	7
Other	8	5	9	3
N =	(54)	(47)	(31)	(26)

[a]Based on the question, "If you have to draft a candidate to run in an election, which of the following arguments do you find most effective?"

[b]The percentages are based on responses for the three most effective incentives and, therefore, do not add up to 100 per cent.

from within the party, this finding is not surprising. Duty-conscious and unambitious partisans are the ones who most likely view this office as a relatively short stint of service that "somebody" must perform in order to help insure the health of the local party. On the other hand, the self-recruited, politically-ambitious chairman should tend to continue to serve under two general conditions: (1) until he gets a favorable opportunity to achieve further office goals (in the party organization or in a public election); or (2) until he perceives that the available opportunities for further office are unfavorable or will not yield the expected values placed upon them.[30]

The county leaders were asked about their past political experiences as office-holders and about their intentions to run for some future public office. In Table 8, the West Virginia chairmen have both previously held and sought public office to a greater degree than their counterparts in Virginia. Sixty percent of the West Virginians in 1966 had sought public elective office but this figure dropped off to 40% by 1970. Despite this decline, the interstate differences may indicate that the longer-established party organizations in West Virginia are more hierarchical and that, for the ambitious activist, upward mobility tends to come in deliberate and graded steps. Conversely, the data on the younger party organizations in Virginia can be interpreted to reflect greater organizational access and less rigid opportunities for political careers.[31] In regard to future intentions to run for office, the number of chairmen with such aspirations never reaches a majority.

TABLE 8

POLITICAL CAREERS AND ASPIRATIONS
OF COUNTY CHAIRMEN BY STATE AND YEAR[a]
(in percentages)

Political Career Choices	Virginia 1966	Virginia 1970	West Virginia 1966	West Virginia 1970
Held public office	16%	21%	28%	22%
Previously sought public office	31	33	60	40
Intends to run for public office	39	33	40	28
N =	(104)	(86)	(40)	(30)

[a]Percentages represent positive responses by state and year and therefore, columns do not add to 100%.

The pattern in both states from 1966 to 1970 reflects a diminishing tendency to run for further office.[32]

The description of this pattern of ambition can be enhanced by relating it to the political structural factor of size of community. Black (1972) argues that achieving political office in places of large population generally is more costly than in places where the population is low. Consequently, urban activists (who usually make a larger investment in the attainment of their political position) should be "pulled" further into an upwardly mobile political career sequence than rural activists.[33]

An analysis of the data in Table 9 generally confirms this hypothesis with the exception of the West Virginia chairmen in 1970.[34] Once again, the fact that 7 or 8 urban chairman do *not* intend to seek public office may reflect a tendency in some of West Virginia's urban Democratic strongholds to recruit a less ambitious and a more realistic and organization-oriented set of grassroots leaders.

The pattern of development of these bivariate relationships from 1966 to 1970 upholds the initial univariate finding (see Table 8) that showed a tendency toward recruiting less ambitious chairmen. A notable exception to this pattern occurs among the ambitious chairmen from urban places in Virginia. They show an increase from 35% in 1966 to 56% in 1970.

Self-Definitions of the County Chairman Role

For purposes of this study, a role refers to the appropriate set of attitudes and behaviors expected of an individual occupying a particular status or position (Newcomb, 1950: 280; Thomas and Biddle, 1966: 22-45; Wright, 1971). Given this definition, the party leader appears to have considerable private flexibility in defining his role orientation. This is primarily due to the lack of clear-cut, formal organizational definitions and expectations for local leadership roles.[35] However, certain general role orientations do emerge among the Republican leaders of Virginia and West Virginia.

The local chairmen in both states were asked to describe the job of being chairmen. They were asked to discuss their major functions and duties. The responses were coded into four general categories: activities related to campaigning, winning elections and becoming competitive; party organizational work; activities related to spreading partisan ideological tenets; and participation in nominations. The first two role orientations predominate and warrant some mention. An organization-oriented county chairman is the type who sees his major function as the establishment and administrative maintenance of the efficiency, loyalty, morale, and fairness of the party organizational machinery. The campaign-oriented leader tends to be motivated by the heat of inter-party struggle and defines his role in terms of raising funds, contacting voters, recruiting candidates, and managing the local campaign.

As Table 10 shows, most of the chairmen in both states place their primary role in either the campaign or organizational categories. This corresponds to the general findings in Patterson's (1963) study of county chairmen in Oklahoma and Bowman and Boynton's (1966b) findings on party officials in Massachusetts and North Carolina.

In Virginia, there is a slight increase in the number of county chairmen (from 60% to 68%) who describe their roles in terms of voter-mobilization and electoral competition. In fact, the two campaign activities mentioned by the chairman (90% in both states) as "the most important" were "building a strong two-party system" and "winning elections." Considering the improving but still minority status of the Republican Party in Virginia, this finding is not unexpected.[36] In their efforts to build competitive local parties, the chairmen appear to receive comfort from an almost ideological fixation on the concept of achieving a two-party system. Whether this response represents a tactical "party line" for public consumption or a real belief about the chairman's role is difficult to interpret. The campaign orientation in West Virginia remains constant over the time interval.

TABLE 9

POLITICAL AMBITION AND SIZE
OF COUNTY BY STATE AND YEAR
(in percentages)

Intends to seek public office	Virginia 1966			Virginia 1970		
	Rural	Lesser Urban	Urban	Rural	Lesser Urban	Urban
Yes	24%	49%	35%	19%	43%	56%
N =	(34)	(47)	(20)	(30)	(36)	(22)

Intends to seek public office	West Virginia 1966			West Virginia 1970		
	Rural	Lesser Urban	Urban	Rural	Lesser Urban	Urban
Yes	29%	47%	50%	24%	43%	13%
N =	(17)	(15)	(6)	(15)	(13)	(8)

The second most frequently mentioned type of activity concerns party organizational work. In West Virginia, about a fourth of the chairmen define their primary role in terms of participation in party adminstration, communication and coordination. In Virginia, the officials identifying with the organizational role definition decline slightly over time. However, where the organizational role is mentioned, it is usually done in the context of providing the support for campaign success.

The roles related to ideological activities and nomination processes receive minor mention. However, several of the Virginia chairmen see the development of the Republican Party as providing a vehicle for a conservative revival at all levels of government.[37]

The nature of the relationship between the political environmental variable of party dominance and role orientation has been examined in several other studies.[38] This "party dominance" hypothesis holds that:

> majority party leaders would incline to organization-oriented roles, while minority party leaders would be more campaign-oriented. The majority party has less electoral insecurity, and presumably wants to build and maintain their organization; the minority party needs to win elections and must emphasize campaign-waging. [Althoff and Patterson, 1966: 46].

TABLE 10

SELF-DEFINED ROLE ORIENTATIONS OF
COUNTY CHAIRMEN BY STATE AND YEAR[a]
(in percentages)

Role Definition	Virginia 1966	Virginia 1970	West Virginia 1966	West Virginia 1970
Campaign	60%	68%	55%	58%
Organizational	25	15	28	25
Ideological	10	9	17	17
Nominations	5	8	-	-
Total	100%	100%	100%	100%
N =	(52)	(42)	(21)	(20)

[a]Based on the first response of chairmen to the question: "How would you describe the job of being county chairman--comment on the nature of your office, your duties and party politics in general." The 1970 data includes two incumbents from Virginia and one from West Virginia.

An analysis of the data on the role orientations of the Republican county chairmen from either Republican-dominant, competitive, or Democratic-dominant counties or cities generally does not support this hypothesis.[39] Table 11 shows that the most commonly perceived role is campaign-related regardless of the factor of partisan dominance at the local level. There are some increases in the number of campaign-oriented chairmen in Virginia from 1966 to 1970 but the small number of cases comprising this crude nominal classification precludes any meaningful discussion or analysis. However, the high number of campaign types in the competitive counties may be a reflection of partisan euphoria and enthusiasm from the Republican gubernatorial and other victories in both states over the time period.

Some earlier discussion indicated that West Virginia and especially Virginia were transitional political systems where the Republican Party was becoming a force to be reckoned with. These general findings have shown that more chairmen perceived their roles as campaign-oriented in 1970 than in 1966 and many of the chairmen saw fulfillment of the goal of creating a two-party system as a primary source of their activity. Consequently, one might speculate that the more recently recruited chairmen perceive the possibility of viable Republican compe-

TABLE 11

ROLE ORIENTATIONS OF CHAIRMEN AND COUNTY
PARTY DOMINANCE BY STATE AND YEAR

Role Orientation	Virginia 1966			Virginia 1970		
	Republican-Dominant	Competitive	Democratic-Dominant	Republican-Dominant	Competitive	Democratic-Dominant
Campaign	50%	82%	50%	75%	72%	67%
Organizational	33	13	30	8	16	22
Ideological	17	5	20	17	11	11
Total	100%	100%	100%	100%	100%	100%
N =	(18)	(22)	(10)	(12)	(18)	(9)

	West Virginia 1966			West Virginia 1970		
	Republican-Dominant	Competitive	Democratic-Dominant	Republican-Dominant	Competitive	Democratic-Dominant
Campaign	6	5	-	2	9	2
Organizational	3	3	1	2	2	-
Ideological	-	3	-	1	1	1
Total	(9)	(11)	(1)	(5)	(12)	(3)

[a]The data for Virginia are presented in percentage form and, the West Virginia data, because of the small number of cases, is presented as raw scores. The nominations role was deleted for the same reason.

tition to be more of an emerging reality than did their earlier counterparts.

CONCLUSION

The objective of this investigation has been to identify and describe the Republican county chairmen from Virginia and West Virginia over the period 1966 to 1970. A profile was presented of a portion of the complex of interrelated factors which make up the extensive and informal incentive and recruitment systems of Republican organizations in these states. Social characteristics, political background, incentives to activity, political ambition, and conceptualization of leadership role were utilized to describe the systems and their effects on the selection of particular individuals for party activity and leadership.

In summary, the findings were interpreted to indicate that the local officials of both time periods in these transitional states reflect to a surprising degree the social attributes and community acceptance of leadership elements generally found in competitive or majority party organizations. In many instances, these individuals tended to be those in the productive years of middle age, those with residential longevity in their communities, those drawn from higher status occupations, and those who were well educated. Parental political activity was present for about half of the activists and there was a greater tendency in Virginia toward recruiting greater numbers of chairmen who had Democratic parents or who, themselves, were Democratic defectors. However, the more recent chairmen in both states often reflected gradual shifts toward even high levels of upper status attributes generally found among the "better people" in local communities.

The most common incentives deemed important for party organizational activity were purposive and the officials tended to use purposive incentives when recruiting prospective candidates for public office. The solidary incentive related to party organizational loyalty also was considered important by many chairmen. The frequencies of all the incentives that were considered important remained relatively stable over the period 1966 to 1970. As a group, the officials of both states had little political ambition for further office. However, urban chairmen in Virginia showed an increased tendency over the time period to be interested in political careers. When asked about their position, the officials tended to define their role in terms of activities related to campaigning and winning elections in order to create a two-party system. This was found to be the case regardless of the competitive strength of the Republicans at the local level.

It is hoped that some of the developments noted in this treatment of local party officials have removed some of the mystery surrounding Republican organizational activism in regional locales of these types. A further hope is that this investigation will encourage other scholars to collect party organizational data in time-series form in order to create more sophisticated developmental theories of elite political behavior.

NOTES

1. The more immediate and proximate recruitment activities of party organizations, as Sorauf points out, do not always explain why specific individuals enter party activity. He describes a more elaborate "recruitment system" that provides a more complete description of the recruitment process. The data in this study are inadequate to describe the nature of this dichotomy of proximate stimuli for activity. However, without a more sophisticated index or scale of some type, the unraveling of the chain of personal causality that determines the decision to become a party activist is, at the least, a difficult task. These complex combinations of internal and external social and psychological factors are difficult to measure and can often be difficult to separate in the memory of an activist. In comparing party activists, the effects of external factors like availability and interpersonal contact are often most important but still are a part of a total recruitment and incentive system.

2. Structural factors (e.g., party competition, electoral system, urbanization) in the environment and the internal location and mechanism for recruitment decision (degree of centralization, self-recruitment versus conscription and the role of organized interests) are important variables at this level of analysis. The goal is to better explain the relationship between recruitment outcomes and organizational effectiveness.

3. In line with the argument presented by Bowman and Boynton, the assumption is made that party officials possess minimal levels of political competence and efficacy and certain other ideological and personality characteristics that help predispose them to party activity. See Bowman and Boynton (1966a: 670); Browning (1968: 94-97); and Schwartz (1969: 552-556) for more complete models of recruitment that include these factors.

4. The questionnaire used in this project was almost identical to one used in a study of North Carolina party officials and has been described elsewhere by William Crotty. See Crotty (1966: 44-53). The differences in return rates between Virginia and West Virginia confirm Crotty's contention that an in-state university of reputation will attract a high response rate. Due to the outright refusal of the Democratic state chairman of Virginia to provide a letter of introduction and mailing lists in both years, it was not possible to gather adequate data on Democratic county chairmen. While inclusion of Democrats would provide an important comparative baseline to measure change, the precise study of intra-party variations in patterns of recruitment and activism is considered of comparable importance on its own merits.

5. For a detailed description of the evolution of the political environments in both states, see, for Virginia, Eisenberg (1972: 39-91) and for West Virginia, see Fenton (1957: 82-125). So that this heterogeneity is not over-emphasized, several similarities between these states warrant mention. First, the Republican organizations in both

states have had considerable recruitment and electoral success in mountainous "Civil War Republican" areas of the states. Second, post-World War II industrial relocations brought to both states an influx of middle-class managers and professionals who helped strengthen the Republican organizations especially in urban and suburban areas. The within-state rural to urban relocations of working class voters indirectly also helped the Republicans by disrupting the traditional Democratic statewide organizations in both states. Also, both states can be considered "civic cultures" in regards to party recruitment and participation in general. The party organizations are neither omnipotent nor overly weak. For a discussion of elite recruitment typologies see Patterson and Boynton (1969: 262-273). For more specific details on Republican office-holding strength, see note 30 of this manuscript.

6. Crotty (1967: 672-673) elaborates on this when he states that:

. . . individuals less integrated into the social structure of the community would be more apt to ally themselves formally with the minority party. It is reasonable to assume that social sanctions would be stronger in mitigating against a native resident's association with a permanent out-group in the community—the minority party. The person most immune to such pressures could well be one who is relatively new to the locality, whose traditions and social relationships are not as deeply rooted as someone who grew up on the area, whose value premises may well be different, and who brought his party identification with him from his former place of residence. The local people may expect and tolerate more deviant behavior patterns from an individual not as completely acculturated to local norms.

7. For example, both states in 1966 have almost twice as many college graduates and graduate degree holders among the chairmen than was found in the minority Republican officials in North Carolina. See Crotty (1967). An approximately similar pattern holds when compared with minority leaders in Oklahoma, New Jersey, Kansas and Wisconsin.

8. Marvick identifies them through self-ratings and reputational scores as "key figures" in the organization who have a stronger identification with their party than do the "fringe cadre." See Marvick (1968).

9. Because of the heavy turnover of Republican officials over the time interval in both states (which in itself may be an indicator of change) and the above-mentioned higher social status of the 1966 groups (especially in Virginia), the matter of the social characteristics of those officials retained is not a very helpful datum in examining change. In Virginia, a total of sixteen chairmen (out of 102) serving in 1970 had served in 1966. Seven of these officials could be described as "marginal" social types with lower occupational and educational characteristics. Without going into greater detail, these men tended to be long-term residents of their counties and tended to be older (four out of five were over 55 years of age) but they all came from Democratic-dominated counties where the Republican organizations were very weak and where Republican cadre were probably still difficult to recruit. The other nine chairmen were either college graduates or had higher status occupations (most had both). Eight of the nine came from at least competitive locales. In West Virginia, seven of the thirty-seven chairmen from 1970 previously had served in 1966. Given the longer-established and independent local Republican organizations in West Virginia, this higher percentage of retention is expected. As indicated earlier, local GOP "fiefdoms" still flourish in particular parts of the state and are often represented by officials with long tenure. Four of the incumbents were of marginal status, older and came from heavily Democratic, rural counties. The remaining three upper status chairmen came from competitive locales.

10. This tendency conforms to the general literature on political leadership and to the findings in other studies on grassroots party leaders. For citations to this literature see: Marvick (1968: 1, note 1). See especially: Crotty (1967: 674-675); Bowman and Boynton (1966a: 672); and Patterson (1963: 338-339). In both states, the Republican cadre had much higher levels of educational attainment than the general population. At the lower end of the educational scale, 78 and 87% respectively, of the Virginia and West Virginia general population had only completed high school or less as compared to just 12% of the Virginia chairmen and 25% of the West Virginia chairmen from 1970. At the upper end of the educational range, the county chairmen with college or graduate degrees are seven to eight times more numerous than the comparable proportion in the general public. Source: U.S. Bureau of the Census. General Social and Economic Characteristics (1970, Vol. 1, Parts 48 and 50).

11. A partial explanation of the latter finding can be found in a recent study of Democratic voters in West Virginia in which the high political participation of lower socio-economic groups is examined and viewed as a feature of that state's political culture. See Johnson (1971). Johnson convincingly argues that organized involvement has become incorporated into the political culture and style of West Virginia politics and has resulted in high levels of participation. The efforts to unionize miners in West Virginia during the 1920's led to an encouragement of the lower socio-economic group, i.e., the "working man," to become active in politics. This cultural variable may be active in the Republican party cadre as well, and could be reflected in a relatively high level of chairmen with low educations in both time periods. However, the 1970 Republican chairmen in West Virginia are slightly better educated than the 1966 group.

12. Angus Campbell et al. provide a well-known and useful general explanation of the relationship between age and political interest and activism. They see the twenties as usually an inactive political period that is devoted to the demands of academic, marital and career pursuits. A "settling-in" process occurs in the thirties with children being raised, and occupational and financial stability occurring. During this period of decreased economic pressure, new activities of a social and community nature can be started. Politics is a potential area for such activity. In the forties and early fifties, political participation and interest are high especially when measured by voter turnout. The late fifties and sixties normally bring a diminution of political behavior, most noticeably in activities beyond voting. See Campbell et al. (1960: 493-498).

13. Although generational party defection will be mentioned at a later point in this study, a logical deduction from this finding is that more of the 1970 county chairmen probably had parents who were associated with the majority Democratic Party. As another aside, in 1970, 16% of the Virginia activists as opposed to 5% of those in West Virginia had switched from the Democratic Party. This may be interpreted to indicate that the development of the GOP is in a more recent and dynamic stage in Virginia. Also, both Patterson and Crotty found that the minority party in Oklahoma and North Carolina attracted more people to county chairmenships who were not native sons than did the majority party. See Patterson (1963: 382-383) and Crotty (1967: 673-674).

14. The professional, manager-sales, category accounts for 74% of the 1970 Virginia chairmen while the category comprises only about 32% of the general population. The lower-status occupations show a similar (in magnitude) degree of under-representation among the Virgina chairmen. In West Virginia, the general pattern is about the same. Source: U.S. Bureau of the Census. General Social and Economic Characteristics (1970, Vol. 1, Parts 48 and 50).

15. There are two other explanations: (1) Max Weber's concept of "role dispensabil-

ity," i.e., the flexibility in time and other characteristics of an occupation that enables the individual to get direct and indirect benefits from entering active politics; and (2) Herbert Jacob's notion of the importance of "brokerage occupations," i.e., an occupational role that places its practitioners into a bargaining role where they deal with outsiders (non-subordinates) and try to reach mutually satisfying agreements. Jacob sees many people with "political" personalities going into such occupations.

The data in this study show that skills associated with the brokerage role are not particularly critical to holding the post of county chairman. The fact that about half of the professionals in both states are engineers (a non-brokerage job) may account for this finding.

16. Although the data are not shown, urban chairmen outnumber rural chairmen in higher status-occupations (62% to 37%). Rural counties tend to attract more "middle" status people (small businessmen, merchants, supervisors, foremen, large farm owners, retired military types) to the county chairmanship. This may be the case in Virginia because the Democratic Party is dominant in a greater number of rural counties than urban and is better able to attract "higher" status people. However, of greater significance is the fact that 75% of the Republican chairmen with low occupational status serve in Democratic-dominated counties. In West Virginia, no substantial differences were found in the occupational distribution over time when the urban-rural distinction was used as a control variable. There is a slight tendency for chairmen with low occupational status to serve more often in rural counties and for higher status officials to serve in suburban and urban counties. Sixty-eight percent of these low status officials were serving in Democratic-dominant counties.

17. In West Virginia, rural counties were defined as having 20,000 or less; lesser urban counties were classified using the 20,001-59,999 category; and urban counties were defined as places with a 60,000 or greater population. The fact that Virginia is predominantly urban and West Virginia is predominantly rural necessitated the use of two criteria. It was felt that this procedure would provide the most accurate classification. In Virginia, rural counties were defined as counties with a city of 3,500 or less; lesser urban counties were defined as counties with cities of 3,500 or more and urban counties and independent cities were defined as areas falling in the Standard Metropolitan Statistical Area category established by the U.S. Census Bureau.

The analysis resulted in too many extremely small or empty cells so the table is not shown. In Virginia, the chairmen in the professional, manager-sales category increased by 12% in rural counties (N=35), 11% in lesser urban counties (N=44), and remained almost static in urban cities and counties (N=19 in 1966 and 23 in 1970). In West Virginia, the comparable figures are 7% in rural counties (N=18 and 15), 10% in lesser urban counties (N=15 and 12), and 18% in urban counties (N=7 and 8). Another interesting phenomenon may be taking place in the most rural areas of West Virginia where the blue collar chairmen (4 in 1966) have disappeared. No statistically significant differences obtained when age, education and residence were controlled by urbanization or party dominance.

18. County party dominance was measured by the percentage of the gubernatorial vote won by each *major* party in 1965-69 (Virginia) and 1964-68 (West Virginia). When either party attracted 60% or more of this vote in each year, it was considered dominant. If the margin of victory was 19% or less, i.e., less than a 60-40 split, the county or city was classified as competitive. The results of this classification system correlate with another system using vote percentage and contesting frequency of elections to the House of Representatives between 1964 and 1970 but it was felt that the former

attempt better captured the political realities in the two transitional states. It is important to remember that seven of the ten Virginia U.S. House seats currently are held by Republicans but the Democrats hold more than two-thirds of the state legislative seats. The Republicans have done better at the legislative level in West Virginia but have had problems in presidential, congressional and top state elections. Both states currently have Republican governors and in 1972 Virginia elected a Republican to the U.S. Senate.

Some of the weaknesses in using only gubernatorial elections for describing competitiveness are known to the author but the present scheme is deemed adequate for this study. For other attempts at classification see the following: Eulau (1957); Gold and Schmidhauser (1960); Stern (1972).

19. For a similar interpretation of the recruitment of Republican local officials in a North Carolina community, see Bowman and Boynton (1966a: 676).

20. For empirical verification of the fact that voters in the white South have been steadily moving away from the Democrats (though not toward the Republicans because of Wallace) since 1956 see Axelrod (1972: 14-16).

21. In attempting to describe incentives for party activism, I accept the theory of motivation developed by McClelland et al. and general theories of rational choice, both of which consider choice as a function of goals (or utility) and expectations. Incentives serve as measures of the utility of certain satisfactions and family political interest and activity act as indicators of expectations of attaining these satisfactions in the party organization. See McClelland et al. (1953); Atkinson (1964); Browning (1968: 99).

22. This finding conforms to the results found in the general literature on incentives to party activism. Wilson and others identify the "amateur" orientation and amateur organizations (of a reform nature) as being based on purposive incentives. See Wilson (1962: 164). Another group of studies examines the maintenance of purposive incentives from initial to sustained activism. Along with Wilson, Conway and Feigert (1968), found a shift over time to more personalized and instrumental motivations. Others have found evidence that shows the maintenance of purposive incentives from initial to sustained party activism. See Ippolito (1969) and Browder and Ippolito (1972). The inadequacy of the data on sustaining motivations in this study makes it impossible to present findings that speak to this question. Another study used a factor analysis to test Wilson's typology and the categories were found to be grouped as they had been categorized prior to data collection. See Parker (1972).

23. Salisbury points out a similar explanation when he discusses the effects of socialization on party activism. He cites "highly politicized" families as agents for the "habitual" activism of offspring. See Salisbury (1965-66: 562-564).

24. One can only speculate that Republican electoral successes (especially at the gubernatorial level) during this period may account for some of this change.

25. A number of others factors including age, desire to continue in office, tenure in office and nature of first contest for office were cross-tabulated with the incentives but few major differences were found between continuation in office and party loyalty. This was obtained in both states and the tendency was for a slightly greater proportion of activists desiring to continue in office to rate this incentive as important. There was a slight increase in this group from 1966 to 1970.

26. An earlier study of both Republican and Democratic local officials in Massachusetts and North Carolina reports a similar ordering of the incentives. The authors add that this might also indicate the unavailability of material incentives at the grassroots levels of party structures. See Bowman et al. (1969). They also found that continuing

officials rated party loyalty higher than terminal officials.

27. It is assumed that "self-starters" who essentially recruit themselves probably rely more heavily on incentives related to concern for issues or material incentives related to ambition.

28. This was found in another study where a local recruitment process was described as "the maintenance of a generally amateur orientation." See Browder and Ippolito (1972: 170-172). Crosstabulations between the chairmen's motives and the incentives they used as recruiters revealed almost no direct evidence that a similar pattern was present in Virginia or West Virginia. Descriptions of either reform group membership or general attitudinal components (besides the motivational components) are other ways to describe the existence of the "amateur" orientation. See Soule and Clark (1970) for an explanation of amateurism as a multi-dimensional set of attitudes about party politics.

29. Schlesinger has formulated a well-known approach to recruitment and leadership in the form of a deductive theory of ambition. The linchpin of his conception is that political leaders rationally respond to the goals of office as determined by the availability of the political "opportunities" found in political structures. This section examines the possibility that some local party officials may see the county chairmanship as a springboard to wider political careers. See Schlesinger (1966); Edinger (1967). For an examination of political ambition and recruitment that emphasizes the importance of environmental and immediate factors in political career decision-making, see Black (1972).

30. Among the chairmen in 1966, 85% were unopposed in West Virginia. By 1970, these figures had declined to 70% in Virginia and increased slightly to 73% in West Virginia.

31. For a similar interpretation of data from Oklahoma, see Sorauf (1968: 92).

32. Whether or not these findings represent a tendency to recruit less upwardly-mobile and career-oriented officials, and more organization-oriented "turn-takers" cannot be directly answered by this data.

33. Black points out that size of community and degree of electoral competitiveness may have an important effect on the decision to pursue political office because they help determine the relative costs of candidates seeking office. He discusses the notion that these structural factors are often related to the resources (like money, time, effort, etc.) that ambitious individuals have to spend on achieving political office. He finds that the size of a place is also related to the degree of electoral competition. Larger city elections tend to be more closely contested than those in smaller communities. See Black (1972: 146-157) for an explication of this argument.

Analysis of the relationship between political ambition and degree of competition in the case of the Republican county chairmen weakly confirms Black's hypothesis but there were only slight differences over time so the data will not be shown. Needless to say, in the case of the county chairmen, other costs may be attached to further office-seeking related to animosities, hostilities, and anxieties resulting from prior decisions made at the chairmen level. These factors can result because of conflicts both in local Republican parties and in the relationship between the local chairmen and district and state party officials. Of course, knowledge obtained from experiences in painful or unsuccessful campaigns against the Democrats can result in awareness of the probability of similar psychological costs occurring for the aspiring chairman.

34. The very small number of cases in the urban category in West Virginia in both 1966 (N=6) and 1970 (N=8) necessitates only a cautious and tentative interpretation of the West Virginia data.

35. Poor communication is another factor. Wright points out that the "poor communications of role expectations is probably the result of a combination of factors, including the lack of clarity of formal role definitions and expectations, the often poorly developed party communications channels, and the volunteer character and high turnover rate of party activists." Wright (1971: 346). The lack of effective sanctions is another factor that helps explain the often idiosyncratic self-definitions of their roles by local party chairmen. Also, see the discussion in Eldersveld (1964).

36. Patterson found that the Oklahoma chairmen tended to be more campaign-oriented if they were in the minority party, see Patterson (1963: 352). The effects of competition will comprise the last portion of this section.

37. Several chairmen indicated that strengthening causes like the defense of property rights against the national Democrats and the control of "leftist extremism" were enhanced when conservatives filled party leadership positions.

38. See Lane (1959: 307) and Patterson (1963: 348-52). These studies compared differences between the two major parties but its application in this study, of course, examines leaders of a single party in different states and at different times. Also, the hypothesis is usually supposed to apply to less- or greater-than purely competitive situations. In this study, the decision was made to analyze the role orientations of chairmen in competitive situations because of their potential importance to the degree of Republican success in both of these transitional systems.

39. Bowman and Boynton (1966b) also found no consistent patterns. Eldersveld (1964) found another pattern: precinct leaders of both parties tended to be most campaign-oriented in the "sure" Republican precincts. Ippolito found data supporting a reversal of the original hypothesis in his examination of Naussau County executive committeemen. He found that minority Democrats were more organization-oriented and the majority Republicans were more campaign-oriented. See Ippolito (1969b). It is clear that the testing of the dominance hypothesis has resulted in a variety of patterns. This may, in part, be due to the lack of more standardized criteria for classifying leaders as to role orientation and to the particular contextual effects found in the political settings of diverse communities and states.

REFERENCES

ALFORD, R. and H. M. SCOBLE (1968) "Sources of local political involvement." American Political Science Review 62: 1192-1206.

ALTHOFF, P. and D. BRADY (1972) "Toward a causal model of the recruitment and activities of grassroots political activists." Social Science Quarterly 53 (December): 598-605.

ALTHOFF, P. and S. C. PATTERSON (1966) "Political activism in a rural county." Midwest Journal of Political Science 10 (February): 39-51.

ATKINSON, J. W. (1964) An Introduction to Motivation. Princeton: D. Van Nostrand.

AXELROD, R. (1972) "Where the votes come from: an analysis of electoral coalitions, 1952-68." American Political Science Review 66 (March): 14-16.

BARBER, J. D. (1965) The Lawmakers. New Haven: Yale University Press.

BLACK, G. S. (1972) "A theory of political ambition: career choices and the role of structural incentives." American Political Science Review 66 (March): 144-159.

BOWMAN, L. and G. R. BOYNTON (1966a) "Recruitment patterns among local party officials: a model and some preliminary findings." American Political Science Review 60 (September): 667-676.

--- (1966b) "Activities and role definitions of grassroots party officials." Journal of Politics 28 (February): 121-142.

BOWMAN, L., D. IPPOLITO, and W. DONALDSON (1969) "Incentives for the maintenance of grassroots political activism." Midwest Journal of Political Science 13 (February): 126-139.

BROWDER, G. and D. IPPOLITO (1972) "The suburban party activist: the case of southern amateurs." Social Science Quarterly 52 (June): 168-175.

BROWNING, R. D. (1968) "The interaction of personality and political decisions to run for office: some data and a simulation technique." Journal of Social Issues 24 (July): 93-109.

BUCHANAN, W. (1970) Understanding Political Variables. New York: Merrill.

CAMPBELL, A., P. E. CONVERSE, W. P. MILLER, and D. E. STOKES (1960) The American Voter. New York: John Wiley and Sons, Inc.

CLARK, P. B. and J. Q. WILSON (1961) "Incentive systems: a theory of organizations." Administrative Science Quarterly 4 (September): 129-166.

CONSTANTINI, E. and K. H. CRAIK (1969) "Competing elites within a political party: a study of Republican leadership." Western Political Quarterly 22 (December): 879-903.

CONWAY, M. M. and F. B. FEIGERT (1968) "Motivation, incentive systems, and the political party organization." American Political Science Review 62 (December): 1159-1173.

CROTTY, W. J. (1966) "The utilization of mail questionnaires and the problem of a representative mail rate." Western Political Quarterly 19 (March): 44-53.

CROTTY, W. J. (1967) "The social attributes of party organizational activists in a transitional political system." Western Political Quarterly 20 (September): 669-681.

CROTTY, W. J. [ed.] (1968) Approaches to the Study of Party Organization. Boston: Allyn and Bacon.

CUTRIGHT, P. and P. N. ROSSI (1958) "Grass roots politicians and the vote." American Sociological Review 33: 171-179.

EDINGER, L. J. [ed.] (1967) Political Leadership in an Industrialized Society. New York: John Wiley and Sons.

EISENBERG, R. (1972) "Virginia: the emergence of two-party politics," pp. 39-91 in W. C. Havard (ed.) The Changing Politics of the South. Baton Rouge: Louisiana State University Press.

ELAZAR, D. J. (1966) American Federalism: A View from the States. New York: Thomas Y. Crowell.

ELDERSVELD, S. J. (1964) Political Parties: A Behavioral Analysis. Chicago: Rand, McNally and Co.

EULAU, H. (1957) "The ecological basis of party systems." Midwest Journal of Political Science 1 (August): 125-135.

FENTON, J. H. (1957) Politics in the Border States. New Orleans: The Hauser Press.

FLINN, T. A. and F. M. WIRT (1965) "Local party leaders: groups of like minded men." Midwest Journal of Political Science 9 (February): 77-98.

GLUCK, P. R. (1972) "Research note: incentives and the maintenance of political styles in different locales." Western Political Quarterly 25 (December): 753-760.

GOLD, D. and J. SCHMIDHAUSER (1960) "Urbanization and party competition: the case of Iowa." Midwest Journal of Political Science 4 (February): 62-75.

GRASSMUCK, G. L. (1964) "Emergent Republicanism in the South." A paper delivered at the 1964 Annual Meeting of the American Political Science Association, Chicago.

HIRSCHFIELD, R. S., B. E. SWANSON, and B. D. BLANK (1962) "A profile of political activists in Manhattan." Western Political Quarterly 15 (September): 489-506.

HOFSTETTER, C. R. (1972) "Organizational activists: the bases of participation in amateur and professional groups." A paper presented at the 1972 Annual Meeting of the American Political Science Association, Washington D.C. (September).

HUNT, A. L. and R. E. PENDLEY (1972) "Community gatekeepers: an examination of political recruiters." Midwest Journal of Political Science 16 (August): 411-438.

IPPOLITO, D. S. (1969a) "Motivational reorientation and change among party activists." Journal of Politics 31 (November): 1098-1101.

--- (1969b) "Political perspectives of suburban party leaders." Social Science Quarterly 49 (March): 800-815.

JACOB, H. (1962) "Initial recruitment of elected officials in the U.S.—a model." Journal of Politics 24 (November): 703-716.

JOHNSON, G. W. (1971) "Research note on political correlates of voter participation: a deviant case analysis." American Political Science Review 65 (September): 768-776.

KESSELMAN, M. (1973) "Recruitment of rival party activists in France: party cleavages and cultural differentiation." Journal of Politics 35 (February): 2-44.

LANE, R. E. (1959) Political Life. Glencoe, Ill.: Free Press.

MCCLELLAND, D. C., J. W. ATKINSON, R. A. CLARK, and E. L. LOWELL (1953) The Achievement Motive. New York: Appleton-Century-Crofts.

MCCLOSKEY, H. and H. E. DAHLGREN (1959) "Primary group influence on party loyalty." American Political Science Review 53 (September): 757-776.

MARVICK, D. (1968) "The middlemen of politics," in W. Crotty (ed.) Approaches to the Study of Party Organization. Boston: Allyn and Bacon.

MARVICK, D. and C. NIXON (1961) "Recruitment contrasts among rival campaign groups," pp. 193-217 in D. Marvick (ed.) Political Decision-Makers. New York: The Free Press.

MILBRATH, L. (1965) Political Participation. Chicago: Rand McNally.

NEWCOMB, T. M. (1950) Social Psychology. New York: The Dryden Press.

PARKER, J. (1972) "Classification of candidates' motivations for first seeking office." Journal of Politics 34 (February): 221-268.

PATTERSON, S. C. (1963) "Characteristics of party leaders." Western Political Quarterly 16 (June): 332-352.

PATTERSON, S. C. (1968) "Political cultures of American states." Journal of Politics 30 (February): 187-209.

PATTERSON, S. C. and G. R. BOYNTON (1969) "Legislative recruitment in a civic culture." Social Science Quarterly 50 (September): 243-263.

POMPER, G. (1965) "New Jersey county chairmen." Western Political Quarterly 18 (March): 186-197.

PREWITT, K. (1965) "Political socialization and leadership selection." Annals of the American Academy of Political and Social Science 361: 569-582.

PREWITT, K. (1970) The Recruitment of Political Leaders: A Study of Citizen Politics. Bobbs-Merrill Co.

RANNEY, A. (1965) "Parties in state politics," pp. 61-99 in H. Jacob and N. Vines (eds.) Politics in the American States: A Comparative Analysis. Boston: Little, Brown and Co.

ROSSI, P. H. and P. CUTRIGHT (1961) "The impact of party organization in an industrial setting," pp. 81-116 in M. Janowitz (ed.) Community Political Systems. Glencoe, Ill.: The Free Press.

SALISBURY, R. H. (1965-66) "The urban party organization member." Public Opinion Quarterly 29 (Winter): 553-561.

SCHLESINGER, J. A. (1966) Ambition and Politics: Political Careers in the United States. Chicago: Rand McNally.

--- (1955) "A two-dimensional scheme for classifying the states according to the degree of inter-party competition." American Political Science Review 49 (December): 1120-1128.

SCHWARTZ, D. C. (1969) "Toward a theory of political recruitment." Western Political Quarterly 22 (September): 552-571.

SEAGULL, L. M. (1970) "The emergence and persistence of Republicanism in the deep and rim South." A paper delivered at the sixty-sixth annual meeting of the American Political Science Association, Los Angeles.

SEARS, D. O. (1969) "Political behavior," pp. 370-399 in G. Lindsey and E. Aronson (eds.) Applied Social Psychology, Vol. 5, The Handbook of Social Psychology. Reading, Pa.: Addison-Wesley.

SELIGMAN, L. G. (1961) "Political recruitment and party structure." American Political Science Review 55 (March): 77-86.

SNOWISS, L. M. (1966) "Congressional recruitment and representation." American Political Science Review 60 (September): 627-639.

SORAUF, F. J. (1968) Party Politics in America. Boston: Little, Brown and Company.

SOULE, J. W. and J. W. CLARKE (1970) "Amateurs and professionals: a study of delegates to the 1968 Democratic national convention." American Political Science Review 64 (September): 888-898.

STERN, M. (1972) "Measuring inter-party competition: a proposal and a test of a method." Journal of Politics 34 (August): 889-904.

THOMAS, E. J. and B. J. BIDDLE (1966) "Basic concept for classifying the phenomena of role," pp. 22-45 in B. Biddle and E. Thomas (eds.) Role Theory: Concepts and Research. New York: John Wiley and Sons.

U.S. Bureau of the Census (1970) General Social and Economic Characteristics, Part 48, Virginia and Part 50, West Virginia. Washington, D.C.: Government Printing Office.

WATTS, T. (1968) "Application of the attribution model to the study of political recruitment," pp. 307-340 in W. Crotty (ed.) Approaches to the Study of Party Organization. Boston: Allyn and Bacon.

WILSON, J. Q. (1962) The Amateur Democrat. Chicago: University of Chicago Press.

WRIGHT, W. E. (1971) "Comparative party models: rational-efficient and party democracy," pp. 17-54 in W. Wright (ed.) A Comparative Study of Party Organization. Columbus, Ohio: Charles E. Merrill.

ZEIGLER, H. and M. A. BAER (1968) "The recruitment of lobbyists and legislators." Midwest Journal of Political Science 12 (November): 493-513.

THOMAS H. ROBACK is an Assistant Professor of Political Science at the Virginia Polytechnic Institute and State University. He received his B.A. and Ph.D. from Florida University (1969), and is currently directing the National Republican Leadership Project. His field of interest includes American political party organization and ideology, and he has authored several papers in this area.

A Better Way of Getting New Information

Research, survey and policy studies that say what needs to be said—
no more, no less.

The Sage Papers Program

Eight regularly-issued original paperback series that bring, at an unusually
low cost, the timely writings and findings of the international scholarly
community. Since the material is updated on a continuing basis, each
series rapidly becomes a unique repository of vital information.

Authoritative, and frequently seminal, works that NEED to be available

- To scholars and practitioners
- In university and institutional libraries
- In departmental collections
- For classroom adoption

Sage Professional Papers

COMPARATIVE POLITICS SERIES
INTERNATIONAL STUDIES SERIES
ADMINISTRATIVE AND POLICY STUDIES SERIES
AMERICAN POLITICS SERIES
CONTEMPORARY POLITICAL SOCIOLOGY SERIES
POLITICAL ECONOMY SERIES

Sage Policy Papers

THE WASHINGTON PAPERS

Sage Research Papers

SAGE PUBLICATIONS
The Publishers of Professional Social Science
Beverly Hills • London

Sage Professional Papers in Comparative Politics

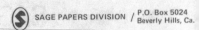

SAGE PAPERS DIVISION / P.O. Box 5024 Beverly Hills, Ca.

PROFESSIONAL PAPER **SUBSCRIPTION** INFORMATION APPEARS ELSEWHERE ON THIS C.

age Professional Papers
n International Studies

or: **Vincent Davis**, *University of Kentucky*
Maurice East, *University of Kentucky*

ents analyses—from many disciplines—of international rela-
s and interactions, foreign policy, international organization,
itical economics on an international level, and various theo-
al and empirical studies in this broad and exciting field.

The Washington Papers *A Sage Policy Papers series*

. . . intended to meet the need for authoritative, yet prompt, public appraisal of the major changes in world affairs.

Commissioned and written under the auspices of the Center for Strategic and International Studies (CSIS), Georgetown University, Washington, D.C., and published for CSIS by SAGE Publications, Beverly Hills/London.

Series Editor: **Walter Laqueur**, *Director of the Institute of Contemporary History (London) and Associate, CSIS, Georgetown University*

Specially commissioned to bring you authoritative evaluations of major events affecting (and affected by) current developments in U.S. foreign policy and world affairs, THE WASHINGTON PAPERS offer timely, provocative, in-depth analyses by leading authorities—who also predict likely future developments and analyze the policy implications of recent trends.

Price Information: Individual papers in the series are available at $2.50 each.
Save on subscriptions: Individuals and institutions can realize substantial savings by entering a subscription order (commencing with Volume I) at the prices given below.

	1 year	2 year	3 year
Institutional	$20	$39	$57
Individual	$12	$23	$33

Outside the U.S. and Canada, add $1 per year to above rates.

Frequency: 10 papers will be published each calendar year—and mailed to subscribers in groups of 3 or 4 throughout the year.

ORDER FORM

Please send the individual papers whose numbers I have listed below:

_____

_____

_____

_____

name _____

institution _____

☐ Please invoice (INSTITUTIONS ONLY) quoting P.O. # _____ (shipping and handling additional on non-subscription orders)

address _____

☐ Payment enclosed (Sage pays shipping charges)

city/state/zip _____

INSTITUTIONAL ORDERS FOR LESS THAN $10.00 AND *ALL* PERSONAL ORDERS *MUST BE PREPAID.* (California residents: please add 5% sales tax on non-subscription orders.)

Please enter subscription(s) to:

☐ Prof. Pprs. in Admin. Policy Studies
☐ Prof. Pprs. in Comparative Politics
☐ Prof. Pprs. in Contemporary Political Soc.
☐ Prof. Pprs. in American Politics
☐ Prof. Pprs. in International Studies
☐ Prof. Pprs. in Political Economy
☐ The Washington Papers
☐ Sage Research Papers

MAIL TO:

 SAGE Publications, Inc. / P.O. Box 5024 Beverly Hills, California 90210

orders from the U.K., Europe, the Middle East and Africa should be sent to Sage Publications Ltd, 44 Hatton Garden, London EC1N 8ER